THE BATTLE
FOR DUNG HILL

THE BATTLE FOR DUNG HILL

Robert Eringer

Illustrated by
James Harper

LONDON

To the Warthogs
(you know who you are)

Published by:

Bedlam Books
13 Heath Street
London, NW3 6TP
Great Britain

In collaboration with:

Bartleby Press
11141 Georgia Avenue
Silver Spring, MD 20902
USA

ISBN: 0-910155-51-8
Printed in China

A harvest moon,
bold and full,
rose low
above Dung Hill.

Two armies gathered,
side by side,
each ready
for the kill.

Side right,
a bunch of
rag-tag loonies,
led by Nerdy Turd . . .

Side left,
the French Foreign
Feces, uniformed in
curd.

The heavens filled
with thick, dark cloud,
a thunderstorm with
drenching rain,

Thus rendering
the fetid hill
a battleground
for the insane.

Its slopes,
so steep,
now slippery
and wet,

Who might
win,
an even bet.

The Feces, commanded
by Colonel Crappeur,
A be-medaled
Napoleon sort.

Behind him,
Royal Poo-poohs,
waved regally
from the fort.

Including old
Von Sphincter,
the eldest of
the Court.

A Turkish turd
named
Mustafa Ca-ca,

The Colonel's
right-hand
clart,

Signaled an advance,
sword-raised,
with a piercing
high-pitched
fart.

Up they charged
through compost,

these military
craps.

Their goal,
to plant their flag
upon the peak of
rank Dung Hill.

The anarchists,
opposing, armed
with stones and
cricket bats,

Were equally
determined to
plant *their* flag,
by iron will.

Their rock band
called THE Y-FRONTS
played their hit,
Stairway to Muck.
Beatniks, hippies,
biker turds —
up the hill they truck.

Watching from
the sidelines,
media poops
from the BBC,

Which stands for
British Bowel Cheezers,
which is really
what they be.

The *Poop Post* was there
as well, and their rival,
The Mucky Times.
To observe and report,
piss and fart,
and poke fun at
my rhymes.

A tail-shot eructed
as both sides met
atop Dung Hill.
It was bloody, nasty,
vicious – leaving many
loos to fill.

Colonel Crappeur had the
upper cheek, thanks
to military might.
But Nerdy's Turds had a
secret plan, not barking
but a bite:

Gastro and his Gurkers,
and their cloud
of poison gas.
They sent the Feces
reeling, reeking,
back up
someone's ass.

Constipation hindered
reinforcements to
the site.
"An enema!" cried
Colonel Crappuer, not
giving up the fight.

Nerdy watched with
patience as he rolled
a joint, some grass.
He put reefer to mouth,
lit a match, took a drag,
flicked his light . . .

And ignited the flatulent gas.

The fumes that night
were fearsome,
Dung Hill blown
to smithereens.
Sewage scudded
everywhere — anyone
for beer and beans?